Study Skills

The Rules

Based on the experience of more than 20 Straight A and First Class students, *The Rules* tell you exactly what you need to do to get the grades you want, while still actually having a life.

First published in 2012 by Effective Study Skills Publications, 5 Demesne Manor, Holywood, BT18 9NW, Northern Ireland. First edition 2011 ISBN 978-0-9568456-2-7

British Library Cataloguing-in-Publication Data: A catalogue record for this book is available from the British Library. Library of Congress Cataloguing-in-Publication Data: A catalogue record for this book is available from the Library of Congress

Printed and bound in the UK by Lightning Source UK, Chapter House, Pitfield, Kiln Farm, Milton Keynes, MK11 3LW.

Study Skills

The

Rules

How to achieve exam success while

still actually having a life

Here is what you need to do

1: Only you can make this happen

2: Find out what they want, and then give it to them

3: Never waste a moment's work

4: Take some extra time to actually understand the work properly

5: Leave enough time for learning

6: Don't just sit reading through your notes – engage with them more actively

7: Don't learn too much, don't learn too little

8: Do some past papers

9: If you don't use a computer you're pretty much nuts

10: Be a worker, not a slacker

11: Keep your work sessions short

12: There is no such thing as the 5 minute break

13: Take days *completely* off

14: Look at your life as a whole

15: Bothering to prepare for class will actually save you time

16: Take a few minutes to review after class

17: Want to know how to improve? ASK

18: Hone your note-taking technique

19: Find the book they haven't told you about

20: When approaching a new topic, try to get a very solid grasp of the absolute basics

21: Use the power of the list

22: Postpone procrastination paralysis

Thanks to...

: Rule One

Only you can make this happen

The very fact that you are reading this kind of book shows that you are taking some of the steps necessary to get the grades you want.

You are taking responsibility for your own success, which is exactly what you need to be doing.

There is a limited amount that your teacher or lecturer can do. For one thing, they usually see you as part of a class. For another, some teachers are much better than others, as we all know.

The only person who can make this all happen is YOU.

: Rule Two

Find out what they want, and then give it to them

Learn how to play the game: If you want to play the game, you need to know the rules of the game. If you don't know what the examiner wants to see, then you can't give it to them.

How do I find out what I need to do?

- **Use past papers** at the beginning of the course. For many people the first time they see an exam paper is when they are doing the exam – this is crazy.
- **Ask your teacher** about what the examiner is looking for, about common mistakes that people make in this subject, and about how you personally can improve.
- **Get relevant Examiners' Reports** from your tutor or look for them yourself on the internet.

: **Rule** Three

Never waste a moment's work

The basic principle: Doing work is tough, so make sure that 100% of it counts directly towards your end result. Be selective – make sure that absolutely all the work you do will be of use either in the exam hall or in coursework that contributes to your final mark.

Don't waste work: If you know that you're not going to prepare a topic for the exam, then you should do the absolute minimum amount of work you can get away with on that particular issue. If work doesn't count directly towards your end result, then try to avoid doing it if at all possible, or just do it quickly and get it out of the way.

EXAMPLE – the class test: Clearly the results of a class test, one that doesn't count towards your end result in the exam, don't really matter. However having a class test is a great opportunity to get your proper notes together that you will use to prepare for the real thing. Therefore you should spend your time doing proper work that will be useful to you long-term for the real exam, rather than scrawling some mediocre notes together just for the sake of doing well in the class test. Spend time making and understanding your notes for the exam that counts, rather than wasting effort on work that is only useful in the very short-term to do well at the class test.

: Rule Four

Take some extra time to actually understand the work properly

Why? <u>Exams aren't just testing WHAT you know about that particular subject. Exams are testing whether you can APPLY what you know.</u> In order to apply what you know, you will need to be able to adapt it to the question that the examiner has asked.   You can only do this if you actually genuinely understand the material.

How to understand something:

- **Ask lots of really simple questions:** What is really going on here? Why does it work this way? What would have happened if certain things had been different?

- **Make connections:** How does this fit in with the themes of the course and with other things I have learnt about? How does this relate to other things that I know about that are currently happening in the world e.g. current political events or scientific developments?

- **Put it into your own words:** Translate difficult concepts into your own simple language that you actually understand. This is another way of forcing yourself to engage actively with the material.

The essence of understanding is simplicity: If you really understand something, then you will be able to express its complex ideas in very simple terms, because you understand the material on the most basic level.

: Rule Five

Leave enough time for learning

Pretty can be pretty useless: You can have the prettiest notes in the world, but they will be completely useless if you can't actually remember them.

Classic mistake: Many people spend far too much time making notes and not enough time learning them and actually understanding them.

Just memorising the material is not enough: You need to be able to REMEMBER it AND to be able to APPLY it to the question asked.

So as well as being able to remember your notes, you need to be familiar with them and to genuinely understand them – otherwise you won't be able to adapt them to the question asked under the time pressure of the exam.

Test yourself to make sure that you really do remember your notes. It is absolutely vital to have an honest and accurate understanding of what you know, and what you don't know.

Practice applying what you know to questions using past papers.

Which subject to work on? Work on your weakest subject until it is no longer your weakest. But be careful not to neglect your stronger subjects.

: Rule Six

Don't just sit reading through your notes – engage with them more actively

Classic mistake: Don't sit passively staring at your notes and hoping that it's going in – it isn't. Just reading stuff is a terrible way of trying to learn it.

Understanding and memory: Taking the time to actually understand your notes is by far the best way of helping you to remember them.

Here are some other techniques:

Summarising forces you to simplify your notes. Test yourself by taking a blank page and trying to write out your summaries.

Drawing diagrams and Spidergrams (use Google images if you don't know what this is) forces you to work out what is really important and makes your brain process the information in a different way.

Explaining the material to someone else, either someone who knows about it or someone who doesn't know about it at all, forces you to actively make use of the material, which is what you will have to do in the exam.

: Rule Seven

Don't learn too much, don't learn too little

Remember Goldilocks: Daddy Bear's porridge was too hot, Mummy Bear's porridge was too cold, but Baby Bear's porridge was just right. So...

Don't learn too little: If you have a choice of how much to learn, make sure that you learn enough topics, because getting caught short is a complete disaster. Make sure that you learn enough detail in each topic (see Past Papers to get an idea of the level required). Also learn an additional "emergency" topic or two in less detail that you can fall back on it if your main topics don't turn up.

But don't learn too much either: There's a real danger of getting bogged down with TOO MUCH detail. Information overload may mean that you lack the flexibility to APPLY what you know in the exam.

: Rule Eight

Do some past papers

Most people don't! Many people don't bother using past papers or else leave it so late that they don't have time to look at them at all. The first time they actually attempt questions without their books in front of them is in the exam itself. Crazy!

Practice makes perfect: Practise questions of the kind that are actually going to be asked in the exam. Allocate time to do this as an essential part of your exam preparation.

Get your tutors to mark your answers if you can persuade them to do so.

Note form can be enough: You don't have to write your answers out in full. Practise planning and applying what you know to the question the examiner has actually asked – that's the important thing.

Practise struggling: It is extremely unlikely that the question in the exam will exactly match the material that you have prepared. Adapting what you know to the question asked is the essence of exam success.

Practise this by doing difficult questions that you have to struggle to answer.

Science essentials: Practising problem questions is particularly important in science subjects. It helps you to learn the material, to find out what you know or don't know, and is an essential skill to acquire.

: Rule Nine

If you don't use a computer you're pretty much nuts

If you don't know how to use a computer you are wasting loads of your own time: Knowing how to use a computer will save you *absolutely enormous* amounts of time.

"Cut and paste" will mean that you don't spend your time writing out the same stuff again and again. This function allows you to create really useful notes extremely quickly.

You'll need to know it soon anyway: When you start working you will be expected to know how to use a computer, so learn now and get all the benefits of knowing how to do so.

Learn how to type: There is little point in having a computer otherwise. Typing unlocks the door to all the advantages that a computer can give you. Just buy a typing book and teach yourself - it'll only take you a few days to master, but will be possibly the most useful thing you ever learn. It is as useful as, for example, knowing how to drive a car.

Software: You need to know Microsoft Word (or equivalent). Powerpoint (for presentations) and Excel (for numbers and graphs) are great as well. You can find loads of amazingly useful instructional videos on YouTube. Take notes. Get a friend to give you a few tips.

: Rule Ten

Be a worker, not a slacker

Quantity really matters: If you want the best results, your general attitude should be that of getting work done from day one. Other people will simply find it difficult to compete with the sheer amount of work that you will have under your belt.

Fitting the work in: Try to get as much work done during the school or university day as possible, so that you can have more time off in the evenings and at weekends. Find some quiet corner where you can do some proper work, and make the most of even short periods of time. The others may be talking crap in the café or study area, but you're really not missing out on that much.

Quality really matters too: Taking lots of time completely off and having fun is absolutely essential if you want to work productively over the course of a term (See Rule Fourteen).

: Rule Eleven

Keep your work sessions short

The 40 minute rule: 40 minutes is the length of time that the human brain can concentrate on any one thing. So do 40 minutes and then take a break. Then come back and do another 40 minutes.

Keep your overall session short: It is rarely worth doing more than three or four of these short sessions in a row.

Oh, and "all-nighters" don't really work for most people: You usually get very little work indeed done after it gets too late, so staying up all night is in reality an extremely inefficient way of working. Not to mention that it often completely obliterates the next day!

: Rule Twelve

There is no such thing as the 5 minute break

Be honest, be realistic: Take at least 10.

Step away from the desk: Don't sit surfing the internet at your computer – this isn't a good break at all. Get outside and go and have a chat with someone to fully distract you from the work that you've been focussing on.

Last thing before taking a break or before finishing for the day plan what you need to do next. Write this down to get it out of your head and so that you don't end up thinking about it when you should be relaxing.

Learn the art of quitting for the day when you are too tired to get any more productive work done. It's better use of your time just to relax properly once it gets to this stage.

: Rule Thirteen

Take days *completely* off

Either work that day or don't work: If you say to yourself that you'll "just do an hour at some point", it will hang over you for the whole day and not allow you to relax properly.

<u>Plan</u> to take that particular day off: Don't waste the entire morning feeling guilty about not working, and then finally decide to take that day off – you've already wasted half of it.

<u>Plan</u> your leisure so that you make the most of it rather than just watching some random crap on TV (although this can occasionally be fun of course).

Last thing you do the day before should be to figure out what work you need to do next and write it down so that this isn't churning around in your head when you should be relaxing.

Look at your life as a whole

The key principle: You can only work effectively if you're feeling fresh.

The vital importance of having fun: You need to be fresh when you come back to hit the books. So don't believe the myth that if you want to do well you can't have fun. In reality the opposite is the truth – you can only do really well if you are having a lot of fun.

So, if you want to get the best results, you need to **create a balanced lifestyle:**

- Take plenty of time off.
- Get plenty of sleep: Naps can definitely work well for some.
- Exercise: Is linked to good mental health, is a great distraction from work, and helps you to get a good night's sleep.
- Eat reasonably healthily so that your body has the fuel it needs to work effectively.
- Plan your leisure so that you don't waste it surfing the internet or watching whatever happens to be on TV.

During exam time: It is vital that you maintain these good habits – now they will stand you in good stead when you need them the most!

The generation game: Are you making the most of the support that your family might be able to offer? Everyone's relationship with their parents and siblings is unique. But they may be more receptive to talking about academic issues than you might think, because hopefully and usually they want you to do well.

Encouraging encouragement: Supportive chat from your family can play a big role in your success. So try not to snap even if you're feeling grumpy.

: Rule Fifteen

Bothering to prepare for class will actually save you time

We've all been there: Unprepared, knowing nothing, bored, and occasionally embarrassed when we clearly don't have a clue. There'll be a lot of catching up to in order to get the grades required.

It's a simple equation: Preparation allows participation which allows learning.

Preparing saves you time: The more you learn during the day, the less work you will have to do in the evenings to get the grades you want, and so the more free time you will actually have.

It's the taking part that counts: Participation requires your brain to actively make use of the material you are coming across. Actively engaging with and – even better – making use of the stuff you are learning is the best way of understanding it. And genuinely understanding the material is the absolute key to doing well at exams (see Rule Four).

Location, location, location: Sit near the front so that the teacher can see you and so that you can contribute when you have something to say.

Ask questions: If you don't understand then say so otherwise you may get left behind. Use your tutor as a resource to further your understanding (and so to improve your grades). Stay at the end to get individual input from your teacher if necessary. Book additional time to meet up with your tutor if this opportunity exists.

: Rule Sixteen

Take a few minutes to review after class

When: The best time to further your understanding of any particular topic is immediately after the class in it.

Why: The ideas are already swirling around in your mind, so "strike while the iron is hot" so that you don't lose the benefit of any connections you have made during that class.

What to do: Tidy up your notes. Borrow someone else's to fill in any gaps. Add your own thoughts and questions in square brackets [like this]. Tidying up will be especially easy to do if you have used a computer to take notes on that class or lecture (Rule Nine).

: Rule Seventeen

Want to know how to improve? ASK

Never stop getting feedback: Many students make the same mistakes time and time again, year after year.

Never stop asking questions: The more questions you ask, and the more answers you listen carefully to, the more likely you are to do well.

After each piece of work that you hand in make sure you get concrete suggestions on how this could be improved. Don't accept some bland comment like "very good" as being enough. Ask for two or three concrete suggestions on how you could have made it better.

After exams: Make the very most of any opportunity to find out how you could have done better. Most people don't!

: Rule Eighteen

Hone your note-taking technique

How not to do it: Don't start reading the material from the beginning taking notes as you are going along, and copying out large chunks of text. With this very PASSIVE approach you will end up with far too many notes to learn for the exam and it will take you ages.

How to do it: ACTIVELY "gut" or "juice" the text, allowing you to get maximum benefit in the minimum time:

- *Find out what the argument is* by looking at the conclusion (or the summary or the introduction).
- *Read headings* within each chapter to get an idea as to how the argument develops.
- *The first line of each paragraph* often "signposts" its contents.

When to take notes: Only start taking your notes AFTER reading the text so that you don't end up copying the same thing out again and again.

The quantity required: Only take what you will be able to remember for the exam. You can always come back for more later.

Referencing: If you need to reference your notes then do this after taking them – it's quicker this way. Here's an example of my personal code (SS/PM/44) = Study Skills, Patrick McMurray, page 44. So, after reading an article, and then taking notes, I use this code to mark where I got the notes from, meaning that if I "cut and paste" the notes into a different order, I'll know where I got them from.

Use a Dictaphone to save time: AFTER you've read and marked a chapter you need to take notes. Go through the chapter with a Dictaphone deciding which of your underlined sections are worth using to form part of your proper notes. If something's worth using then record it on the Dictaphone and then type it all up at the end. It's quicker this way. Dictate in short bursts so that you can type up one little burst and then move on to the next.

Dictaphone mistake to avoid: Don't use the Dictaphone as you're going along on during your first read through the chapter – this way you'll end up with too many notes which is a waste of time.

: Rule Nineteen

Find the book they haven't told you about

The book you need is out there: It is highly likely that there is a book somewhere out there that your teacher or tutor hasn't mentioned to you at all, but that would be EXTREMELY useful if you were able to get your hands on it.

So make sure that you find it: The most important hour's work that you do for any topic is the hour you spend searching around on Amazon and Google to find out what's actually out there on the topic you are about to study.

Here are some examples:

- **Books summarising current debates:** All subjects have areas of current controversy, and there may well be a book or two outlining these. This is exactly the sort of thing you need to know about.
- **Articles summarising books:** Book reviews in journals are particularly useful here because they often both summarise recent contributions

and also comment on them and set them in context, so giving us something interesting to say.

- **"Lit crit":** If you're studying literature then search for works of literary criticism – they tell you exactly the sorts of things you'll need to know for the exam, saving you from having to come up with all your own ideas from scratch.
- **Books that your tutors have written themselves:** Some tutors are very shy about mentioning these (while of course others never shut up about them).

The sort of book you're looking for is: Short, recent and written by someone teaching on that topic at a well-known university.

: Rule Twenty

When approaching a new topic, try to get a very solid grasp of the absolute basics

Get an overview: Before you start a subject get an idea of the bigger picture by Googling around on the internet, reading Wikipedia, or even by reading some children's books on that topic. Yes, you have to be very careful about using information from the internet, but it can provide a useful quick introduction which you can then set aside.

Get the bulk of your notes from one source: Pick one book from which to draw your "fundamental" or "framework" notes on that subject. Using one book means that it won't contradict itself and that all the key ideas are likely to be covered. You need to pick this book very carefully indeed, right at the beginning of the course. Find a shortish book written by an author at a good university. Alternatively you could draw your basic notes from university lectures on that subject, if you they are detailed enough (they often aren't).

Understand your basic notes: Before reading more advanced material make sure that you have got a very firm grasp of the basics. If you don't have a rock solid understanding of the fundamentals then (1) the more advanced material will get confusing and (2) you will end up writing the same points down again, wasting time.

Read some more advanced material only once you have understood your basic notes. Slot your notes from the advanced material into your fundamental notes on that topic.

The Master Document: One way of organising your notes on a topic is to create a single document containing ALL your notes on that subject. Doing so means that you know where all your notes are, and also forces you to think about how it all fits together.

: Rule Twenty-one

Use the power of the list

Stress minimisation: Trying to remember loads of stuff is both stressful and inefficient, so use lists to get yourself organised.

Create two lists: (1) your TODAY list and (2) your LATER list

How to use them: Take just two minutes to plan your day each morning, and to review it each evening. Actively consult your TODAY list during the day to see what you need to do and how you are getting on. Get a calendar and make use of it alongside the lists.

Don't get distracted: It is extremely rare to genuinely have to do something absolutely immediately. When a potential interruption arrives then add it to either your TODAY list or to your LATER list. This means you can stay focussed on what you're doing, and not be distracted. Focus is the most important thing you have in preparing for exams: without focus it will be impossible to achieve understanding.

Making later become today: Keep an eye on your LATER list, and when you judge the time is right allocate a few hours to dealing with the tasks on it, otherwise they will never happen.

: Rule Twenty-two

Postpone procrastination paralysis

Know what you are trying to achieve: What are your goals? Is doing this task going to help you to further these goals? If so, then give it 100%.

Key principle: Get the ball rolling – this allows tasks to create their own momentum.

- **Zero delay:** Do ten minutes' work the day you are given it to get the ball rolling.
- **Do something - anything -** connected with the task. Do the easiest thing you can imagine that will move the project forward.
- **5 minutes is easy:** Set yourself a target of doing just five minutes work related to that task. You'll end up doing twenty – and then you're away!
- **It's not about perfection:** There are usually many different ways of scoring equally highly in any piece of academic work.

: Rule Twenty-three

Languages – say *bonjour* to success

Learning vocabulary:

- **Use the power of your imagination:** EXAMPLE - the German word for bottle is "Flasche". Imagine a bottle made of human flesh, FLASHing on and off. The more vivid the image the more difficult it will be to forget. Note down the image beside the word that you are learning.
- **Learn words as part of sentences:** "Il l'a mis dans le placard". (He put it in the cupboard). Learning the word in context makes it easier to remember, practises your grammar, and allows you to learn it alongside another related new word or two.

Read stuff that you are interested in anyway: If you are interested in fashion then Google around to find a fashion site in the language you're studying.

Listening and speaking are usually 50% of the marks but often aren't practised nearly enough in school. Buy CDs and see if you can get foreign radio or TV programmes over the internet.

: Rule Twenty-four

Sciences - your formula for better grades

Practice, practice, practice: Doing loads of problem questions is absolutely key. Don't cheat. Learn from your mistakes. Write down the principles and tricks you've learned and use this to help revision. Use your time in class to practice – participate.

Diagrams: Converting a problem into visual form forces you to think about it a different way. Alternatively, explaining it to yourself out loud can have a similar effect.

Make connections:

- *Between different weeks' work in the same subject:* How does this week relate to the work you did in that earlier week?
- *Between overlap areas in different subjects* (e.g. aspects of biology and chemistry, chemistry and physics, physics and mathematics).

Don't fall behind: Scientific learning often builds on topics covered in previous weeks, so if you fail to grasp one week's work it can mean that the rest of that course becomes a bit of a mystery.

Learning how to get by: Even if you haven't quite managed to understand WHY something works, you can still learn HOW to do the question in the exam, and still get full marks.

Science essays: Don't let this be your Achilles' heel. Remember to define the scientific terms that you use. Back up what you're saying with examples and evidence, but only take the time to draw a diagram if it is genuinely going to add something to what you've written.

: Rule Twenty-five

Google around for tips

Have a bit of a hunt around: Whatever your subject, half an hour Googling around for tips on technique can be very well spent. Search for "study tips maths" or "history source question technique".

Do it early on: This should be one of your first steps when starting a new module. You never know what resources or forums you'll find that might get you off to a flying start.

Be selective: There is some good stuff on the internet but there is also a lot of complete rubbish written by complete wackos. Look for contributions from people who are at recognised universities, or who are writing for established newspapers.

: Interlude How to write great essays

Answer the question the examiner has actually asked

The secret to writing a good essay is to directly answer the question the examiner has actually asked, rather than the question you wish he had asked instead.

Classic mistake number 1: Spotting a word or two in the question that you recognise and then just vomiting out everything that you know about that particular topic.

Classic mistake number 2: Wheeling out an essay that you have prepared on a related but actually quite different question.

In a nutshell: You need to make use of and ADAPT WHAT YOU KNOW to the question that the examiner has actually asked, rather than the one you wish he had asked. To make a decent effort at answering the question the examiner actually asked requires understanding, thought and planning.

Attack the question: For example, if the question refers to "Conservative success in the twentieth century" then you need to explicitly ask whether the question's idea that the Conservatives were successful is in fact correct. Question the question – don't accept it at face value. Examiners will love it if you give them a bit of a fight, especially if you back up what you're saying with evidence. Doing this shows that you are really engaging with and so answering the question.

Resist temptation: Don't start writing immediately – be strong. Starting to write immediately is very tempting because it allows you to kid yourself that you're actually achieving something. In reality, however, the time you spend planning are the moments when the essay is won or lost.

Don't just charge off: Before you pick up the ball and start running, make sure that you are going to be running in the right direction!

How to structure your essay

Before you start writing: Read the question very carefully indeed. Look very closely at the language used in the question, and try to pick out any key words. Planning is absolutely key.

Introductions:

- In the first couple of sentences EITHER say something explicitly about the particular words used in the question (commenting on their precise meaning and implication) OR say why the particular question asked is interesting and important.
- Then say what your argument is going to be, by using the magic phrase *"This essay will argue that.."*
- Then let the examiner know how your argument is going to be structured, by saying *"It's structure will be as follows... Firstly...Secondly...Thirdly etc"*

The main body of the essay:

- Get stuck straight in to answering the question. Don't waste time waffling around and setting the scene, providing "context" etc.
- You don't need to say "In my opinion". All essays *are* your opinion.
- In each paragraph you should make one big point. Make your point, clarify exactly what you mean (or don't mean), and then back up what you're saying with evidence.

Conclusions:

- Answer the question directly in the light of the argument and evidence that you have included in the main body of the essay.
- Be very clear as to what you think. Take a stand - don't sit on the fence (examiners hate this).
- In the final sentences either ram home your argument, or now take a step back and try to set the contents of the essay in context. This is the only point in the essay when you can use language that is slightly more grand, flowery or expansive.

Advanced essay strategies

Forget "balance", just answer the question: Many people think that you should outline one side of the argument, then the other, and then say which you prefer in the conclusion – this is complete rubbish. Simply answer the question that the examiner has asked, and refer to other people's arguments as necessary in the process of developing your own. Start making your own argument from the very first sentences of your introduction.

Follow the leader: Sometimes you may find someone else's argument convincing. If you are setting out an argument that is very similar, if not identical to theirs, acknowledge that you are doing so by putting their name in brackets (Smith).

Show awareness of opposing arguments, but then quickly rubbish them: The examiner will like to see that you have a definite position and so that you have clearly developed thoughts on the key issues. If someone else takes a different view and it would be odd not to mention it then briefly state their position only to quickly rubbish it by pointing out a key flaw or a piece of evidence that they have overlooked. Doing it this way means that while developing your own argument, you are also "showing awareness of current debates", which will also go down well.

Independent thought is more important than pure originality: It is sometimes thought that all originality is good and that this is a common feature of the best essays – again this is rubbish. As a student how can you be expected to come up with brilliant new ideas about subjects that academics have spent their entire careers studying? Rather than struggling for unobtainable originality, show *independent thought* by giving your personal view and evaluation of their arguments, agreeing or disagreeing with them, and – crucially – providing evidence and argument as to why you are doing so.

Sources: Don't underestimate the importance of familiarity with the original sources (e.g. the actual texts in literature, specific pieces of evidence e.g. inscriptions in ancient history).

Quotations: Carefully select quotations that are multi-purpose e.g. telling you both about Hamlet's character, but also about one of the other key themes of the play.

: Rule Twenty-six

Spit it out!!

Thoughts on how to write effectively:

Keep it simple: Use straightforward vocabulary and keep your sentences nice and short.

Don't be pretentious: Don't try to sound impressive or put on some sort of "style" to make your ideas sound grander than they really are. Clear communication and answering the question are what it's all about.

Spit it out! This isn't a poetry competition. There is often a certain brutality about a really good essay, particularly ones written under the time pressure of an exam.

: Rule Twenty-seven

Coursework: It's a great opportunity but don't go overboard

The normal rule applies: Find out what they want to see, and then give it to them. Ask your teacher what they like to see in the particular kind of work that the coursework involves. Ask them about what mistakes are commonly made. Get as much feedback as you possibly can from them along the way.

Why it's worth nailing it: Doing well at coursework means that you will have less to do in the exam to get an excellent result overall. It's a priceless opportunity to give yourself a bit of a head start.

Why it may not be worth *absolutely* nailing it: Think carefully about how much time you should allocate to the coursework. How many marks is it worth relative the marks at stake in the exam? So if the coursework is worth only, say, 20% with the exam being worth 80%, it may be worth giving correspondingly more time to exam preparation. Don't let the time you spend on coursework get out of hand, meaning that you don't have enough time to spend preparing properly for the exam.

Doing the double: If you have a degree of choice as to what you do the coursework on then try to make your work "count double" by choosing a title that will also help you to prepare for the exam i.e. choose a topic that may also come up in the exam.

Choose the more difficult question: If you really want to impress, then choose a more difficult topic as these give better students more of a chance to shine.

Planning is key: When writing a longer piece of work, it's the thinking and the planning that will get you the highest marks. Don't dive in and start writing before you've taken the time to work out exactly what you're going to say.

: **Rule** Twenty-eight

Get good at presentations

Why? Presentations are increasingly used as a mode of assessment, but most people haven't really had that much experience of doing them.

Practise, practise, practise: The more you have practised your presentation, the more likely you are to do well, it's as simple as that.

Relax: No-one really cares about the content of your presentation or about how you do in it. Think about what you're focussed on while other people are giving their presentations – that's right, nothing. They're just waiting for their turn, or thinking what they're going to have for dinner that night.

Grab the audience's attention: Use a striking quotation or image (sourced from the internet) right at the beginning of your presentation. Explain why it's relevant.

Structure is key: Announce the structure of your presentation explicitly right at the beginning. Is there a question that you are trying to answer? Would it help to say what you are NOT going to be talking about? Defining your presentation this way will give you a sense of purpose.

Don't try to fit too much on any one slide: Less is more. Slides that are crammed with information are confusing and distracting. The slide is merely a springboard for your personal explanation.

Try to avoid using notes: Direct communication is key – this is what presentations are testing. If you think that you might "crash and burn" then have your presentation scripted word for word. Pick a friend on each side of the room to talk to make sure that you vary your focus.

Come to a definite ending: Remind your audience of the question you were trying to answer, and then answer it directly in the light of your discussion. At the very end say "Thank you very much for listening" rather than just grinding to a halt.

: Rule Twenty-nine

Think about who you're hanging around with

Friends are really important: Having as much fun as you can in your time off is essential if you want the highest grades. Relaxing with friends will recharge your batteries and mean that you are motivated when you come back to hit the books. Friends are unquestionably among the very, very most important things in life.

But who are your real friends? In reality there will only be a relatively small number of people that you remain in touch with after leaving school or university. Are you spending too much time talking to people who you won't be in touch with in a year or two's time? Is talking crap with some of these guys keeping you back from getting the grades that could well shape the rest of your life?

: Rule Thirty

Squeeze out another session

Boredom is the enemy: Here's a few ideas on how to squeeze out another session or two that might just make all the difference:

Mix it up (1): Do a session on Literature, but then balance that out with a session of Maths.

Mix it up (2): Use different revision techniques to force your brain to think in different ways (Rule Six)

Mix it up (3): Keep switching location - research shows that this significantly improves concentration.

Short sessions are good, especially for high intensity work like learning. You can achieve a lot in 20 minutes if you put your mind to it.

Use YouTube or Google to help to bring your work to life.

: Rule Thirty-one

Turn up on the right day

It's surprising how many otherwise bright people completely mess up some practical aspect of their set of exams.

In short: Turn up on the right day, having prepared for the exam that is actually being held on that day, having remembered to bring any documentation required, having gone to the bathroom, and then proceed to answer the correct number of questions.

: Rule Thirty-two

Whatever you do, don't muck up your timing

This is really, really important: If you get this wrong then - no matter how clever you are - you're pretty much screwed.

Work out your timings in advance: Know how long you have for each section, and know how long you are going to allocate to planning. Work out at what time you need to start to write your answers. Do the maths for this before going into the exam.

Stick to your schedule like glue: There is no other way.

If you mess up the timing then:

- Try to stay calm. Breathe.
- Make a plan as to where you can get most marks most quickly.
- Switch to note form.

: Rule Thirty-three

Work to minimise your nerves

The brutal truth is that the best way to avoid pre-exam nerves is to have done a serious amount of work in preparation for it.

Nerves are not all bad: They will give you the energy to focus and to write quickly when the time is right. Nerves show that you want it.

Avoid talking to people before or after the exam: Even if you've prepared really well there's too much risk that your confidence will be knocked or that you will get confused or panicked. After the exam, even if you've done really well there will be things that you could have written but didn't.

Get a good night's sleep: Research shows that lack of sleep means that you get nervous more easily.

Pre-live your success: Professional sportspeople very often use visualisation techniques to improve their performance. They spend time imagining themselves performing well in situations that they might initially find difficult. To do this, imagine the scene and your participation within it as vividly as possible, and do so on a regular and repeated basis.

Some wacky little tips: Listening to classical music just before an exam has been shown to temporarily improve IQ, and eating chocolate improves blood flow to the brain.

: Rule Thirty-four

Fight!

In an exam you must never, ever, ever, ever give up.

Everyone else is in the same boat: If you're finding it difficult then everyone else will be too.

Keep yourself in the game: Sometimes examiners make a mistake and set an exam that is too hard, in which case everyone's mark gets bumped up. You can't get your mark bumped up if you have walked out the door.

Crazy as it sounds: Taking a short break in the exam (make it one minute or less) can give you more strength to carry on with the struggle.

: Rule Thirty-five

Get ahead during the holidays

Take lots of time off: Use you holidays to have the most fun possible and to get the maximum rest you can before getting back to work.

But then get ahead: Once you're well rested, why not make use of the holidays to get ahead for next year? Doing this can give you an absolutely huge advantage. A huge head-start is there waiting for you if you can be bothered to just go ahead and grab it.

How to do it: Find out which are the best books to start working on by asking your teacher, by getting reading lists in advance, and by searching around in Amazon and Google to see what's out there.

Spelling : impression management

a lot	independent
accommodation	judgement
address	library
aggressive	licence
consensus	maintenance
definitely	millennium
environment	parliament
experience	privilege
fascist	racist
February	restaurant
fulfilment	separate
	vacuum

: impression management Classic confusions

The principal reason the school's Principal is in charge of the school is because she has an excellent grasp of educational principles.

Unless there is an earthquake, stationery remains stationary.

He quoted the following quotation.

They were where they were, there with their cousins.

The effect of his startling performance in the interview was that it seriously affected his chances of getting that, or for that matter any other, job.

He complimented her on the fact that the colour of her dress complemented her beautiful eyes.

"Criteria" is plural. If there is just one, then it's a "criterion".

He ensured that he had the relevant insurance.

I go to piano practice, where I practise the piano.

She literally exploded!! Unless there has been some extreme and highly unusual chemical reaction, this will not *literally* be the case.

: impression management Grammar

Definitely not worth obsessing about, but it will be noticeable if you make mistakes on the following points:

Pizzas for sale. (No apostrophe if it's just a simple plural). Graham's selling Peter's pizzas.

The monkey is in its cage. It's playing with its friend, the chimpanzee.

They were where they were. Their friends are over there.

The less ice there is, the fewer penguins there will be. (If you can't actually count it, use "less").

Thanks to...

I'd like to say a very big thank-you to all my friends who have contributed towards this book, and who have supported me throughout this project. In particular I'd like to thank: Albertine Davies, Owe Carter, Helena Braun, Eleanor James, Graham Geary, Jeremy and Liz Nuttall, Matthias Oschinski, Aileen and David Smith, Trevor McDevitte, Sally Waples, Paul Broom, Iain Jones, Will Wyman, Nicholas Lawn and Kirk Huff. I'd also like to thank the friends who contributed but who chose to remain anonymous.

Thank you also to my family for their love and support. Thanks very much indeed to my Mum and Dad for proof-reading the entire text. Thanks especially to Emily for being so good to me and for generally putting up with me.

This book is dedicated to my very dear sister Katharine, with my love.

Patrick

About the author

Patrick McMurray studied law at Worcester College Oxford, followed by a Masters degree in Forced Migration in the Department of International Development at the same university. After completing the Legal Practice Course at the College of Law he worked as a solicitor in London and he has also worked in a legal capacity for the Refugee Law Project at the University of Makerere in Kampala, Uganda. One day soon he will complete a further degree in Ancient and Modern History at Queen's University Belfast.

www.ingramcontent.com/pod-product-compliance
Lightning Source LLC
Chambersburg PA
CBHW060709030426
42337CB00017B/2822